anythink

Sir Henry Morgan

Cavendish
Square
New York

Laura L. Sullivan

Published in 2015 by Cavendish Square Publishing, LLC
243 5th Avenue, Suite 136, New York, NY 10016

First Edition

Website: cavendishsq.com

This publication represents the opinions and views of the author based on his or her personal experience, knowledge, and research. The information in this book serves as a general guide only. The author and publisher have used their best efforts in preparing this book and disclaim liability rising directly or indirectly from the use and application of this book.

CPSIA Compliance Information: Batch #WW15CSQ

All websites were available and accurate when this book was sent to press.

Library of Congress Cataloging-in-Publication Data

Sullivan, Laura L., 1974-
Sir Henry Morgan / Laura L. Sullivan.
pages cm. — (True-life pirates)
Includes bibliographical references and index.
ISBN 978-1-50260-203-9 (hardcover) ISBN 978-1-50260-202-2 (ebook)
1. Morgan, Henry, 1635?-1688. 2. Pirates—Great Britain—Biography. 3. Buccaneers—Great Britain—Biography. 4. Caribbean Area—History—17th century. 5. Lieutenant governors—Jamaica—Biography. I. Title.

F2161.M83S85 2015
972.9'03092—dc23
B]

2014015586

Editor: Andrew Coddington
Copy Editor: Cynthia Roby
Art Director: Jeffrey Talbot
Senior Designer: Amy Greenan

Senior Production Manager: Jennifer Ryder-Talbot
Production Editor: David McNamara
Photo Research: J8 Media

The photographs in this book are used by permission and through the courtesy of: Cover photo (beach); Denis Burdin/Shutterstock.com; Cover photo, (engraving), Stock Montage/Archive Photos/Getty Images; Rischgitz/Hulton Archive/Getty Images, 1 and 4 (engraving); vladimir salman/Shutterstock.com, 1; UniversalImagesGroup/Getty Images, 6; Kingston and Port Royal from Windsor Farm, from 'A Picturesque Tour of the Island of Jamaica', engraved by Thomas Sutherland, 1825 (colour litho), Hakewill, James (1778-1843) (after)/Yale Center for British Art, Paul Mellon Collection, USA/The Bridgeman Art Library, 8; Ji-Elle/File:Loutherbourg-Un navire maltais attaqué par des pirates algériens.jpg/Wikimedia Commons, 10; Sir Henry Morgan (gouache on paper), Embleton, Ron (1930-88)/Private Collection/© Look and Learn/The Bridgeman Art Library, 12; Abraham Cooper/The Bridgeman Art Library/Getty Images, 14; Indentured servant agreement between Richard Lowther and Edward Lyurd, 31st July 1627 (ink on paper), American School, (17th century)/Virginia Historical Society, Richmond, Virginia, USA/The Bridgeman Art Library, 16; Historic Map Works LLC and Osher Map Library/Getty Images, 19; Fotosearch/Archive Photos/Getty Images, 21; Print Collector/Hulton Archive/Getty Images, 22; © North Wind Picture Archives, 26; Sir John Hawkins(1532-95) (gouache on paper), Frey, Oliver, (b.1948)/Private Collection/The Bridgeman Art Library, 28; Howard Pyle/ File:Pg 020 - The Sacking of Panama.jpg/Wikimedia Commons, 30; John Michael Wright or studio/File:King Charles II by John Michael Wright or studio.jpg/Wikimedia Commons, 32; Blood transfusion from a dog, from 'Armamentarii Chirurgici' by Johannes Schultes (1595-1645) published in Amsterdam, 1671 (engraving) (b/w photo), Dutch School, (17th century)/Bibliotheque de la Faculte de Medecine, Paris, France/Archives Charmet/The Bridgeman Art Library, 35; meunierd/Shutterstock.com, 36; PRNewsFoto/Captain Morgan/AP Images, 39.

Cover and interior design elements: (pirate map) Vera Petruk/Shutterstock.com; (rope on old paper) Irina Tischenko/Hemera/Thinkstock; (skull and crossbones) Tatiana Akhmetgalieva/Shutterstock.com; (crossed swords) Fun Way Illustration/Shutterstock.com; (old map elements) Man_Half-tube/iStock Vectors/Getty Images; (pirate flag) fdecomite/File:Pirate Flag (6084517123).jpg/Wikimedia Commons; (ship) Makhnach_S/Shutterstock.com; (anchor) File:Anchor Pictogram.svg/Wikimedia Commons.

Printed in the United States of America

Contents

1 A (Mostly) Legal Pirate 5

2 A Bloody Career Begins. 13

3 The Terror of the Spanish Main 23

4 Pirate in Retirement 33

Timeline. 40

Glossary. 42

Find Out More. 44

Bibliography 46

Index 47

About the Author 48

Sʳ HEN: MORGAN

one

A (Mostly) Legal Pirate

All **pirates**, by their very nature, led exceptional lives. Though Sir Henry Morgan certainly had a remarkable and exciting life, it is his death that distinguishes him from almost every other pirate. While the majority of **buccaneers** met a grisly fate swinging from a **gallows** at the end of a hemp rope, Morgan's demise was completely different.

When Morgan died in 1688, he had been happily married for twenty years and settled comfortably on his own grand estate in Jamaica. King Charles II of England had given him a knighthood and appointed

Morgan was one of the few pirates to live a long, successful life.

him lieutenant governor of Jamaica. Other pirates spent their final hours rotting in dank prison cells, but Morgan spent his last days staying up late and enjoying the company of friends. When he died, he was given a dignified funeral, and his body was carried to St. Peter's Church, a church that Morgan had used his wealth to help build. Thousands of people mourned him as a respected and valued member of the community.

A Passion for Greed

Morgan died a well-beloved and honored man, not a criminal. For all that, he is remembered as one of the deadliest pirates to ever sail the seas. In his career, Morgan was the terror of Spanish towns and forts in the Caribbean and Central America. He was not above using the weak and powerless to advance his mission for conquest and gold. In his attack on Portobello, he used women, elderly men, friars, and nuns as human shields to keep the enemy from firing on him. He tortured civilians to discover hidden stores of gold. Despite all this, the English considered him a hero because he committed his terrible acts for their side. He even managed to do it all, more or less, without breaking laws.

The Right Time for Piracy

Morgan started his career at the beginning of what is now known as the **Golden Age of Piracy**. In the 1650s, Europe was coming to the end of a period of war and religious conflict that accompanied the **Protestant Reformation**. The Reformation was a religious split among Christians that occurred in many countries, including Germany and England. By the sixteenth century, many expressed doubts about the authority and teachings of the Catholic Church in Rome and created their own versions of the Christian religion. At times, this split caused violence between countries that remained Catholic, such as Spain, and those that became Protestant, such as England. Even when officially at peace, religious conflicts between countries continued.

Free from war in their homelands, European countries were once again able to pursue their **colonial** interests. The Caribbean and Latin America were particularly attractive, being ideal locations for growing profitable crops, such as tobacco and sugar. Central and South America also promised vast supplies of gold. Spain and France had a head start, but England got a solid foothold with the capture of the island of Jamaica in 1655. The situation was ripe for piracy, for both economic and political reasons.

Port Royal, Jamaica, was known as one of the richest—and wickedest—cities on Earth at the time, thanks to the pirates who visited the busy harbor town.

A Fortune for the Taking

Where do robbers go? They go where the money is. In the second half of the seventeenth century, massive fortunes were being transported by ship across the Atlantic Ocean from the colonies to their home countries. Many pirates began life as honest seamen who filled the increased demand for sailors to help carry out the booming trade. They might have been crewmembers on merchant ships, or even mates in the Royal Navy, grueling professions that rarely made anyone rich. An **ordinary seaman** in the navy earned nineteen shillings a month, while an **able seaman** made twenty-four shillings. A merchant sailor usually made a little more. The Royal Navy would **flog** its enlisted crew for the slightest mistake. Private captains could treat their crew even worse.

Some of these sailors were no doubt tempted by the seemingly easy pickings of piracy. Others were captured by pirates, and given no choice but to sign on as crewmembers. Life was more egalitarian, or equal, on a pirate ship. Most pirates even had their own code, called the **articles of agreement**, which not only laid down the law aboard-ship, but also gave the pirate crew rights to **booty**, fair treatment, and even a sort of health insurance in case of injuries.

Pirate or Privateer?

Politically, relations between England and Spain (and between England and France, and England and the Netherlands) were tense during the seventeenth century. Though supposedly at peace on their home continent, they were constantly squabbling for territory and the accompanying riches in the New World. Most European nations were in bad shape. The Thirty Years' War had led to plague and famine that killed half of the population of Germany. Spain was miserably poor, and England was just emerging from a civil war and the military dictatorship of Oliver Cromwell. They all needed the money that new territory could bring, and even though pieces of paper declared them officially at peace, soon new pieces of paper would allow sea captains to wage semi-legal wars of their own. These notorious papers were known as **letters of marque**.

A letter of marque made the difference between a pirate and a **privateer**, and sometimes (though not always) the difference between a pardon and execution by hanging. If a privateer was captured, he was generally imprisoned, but if a pirate was caught, he was tried and killed.

Also known as a "letter of marque and reprisal," this document was issued by a nation's government. The king or queen usually issued a letter of marque, though colonial governors could sometimes grant them. They gave private ship owners and sea captains the authority to attack vessels belonging to other countries. The ships would be captured, the cargo taken, and (in theory) all of it would be turned over to the crown. After that, the ship owner and crew split the proceeds with the government. Often, though, privateers acted almost exactly as real pirates, capturing and sacking other ships and divvying the proceeds among themselves.

Barbary pirates, or corsairs, hunted for treasure ships off the North African coast and in the Mediterranean Sea.

Sir Henry Morgan is often remembered as a pirate, but he was technically a privateer. The English government granted him special permission to attack Spanish ships, towns, and forts. In doing so, he helped England expand its colonial power in the Caribbean and **Spanish Main**. At the same time, Morgan accumulated tremendous personal wealth.

A Pirate By Any Other Name

There are many terms for a person who engages in seagoing attacks. Some are considered synonyms, some depend on location, and some can mean the difference between guilt and innocence, life and death.

Buccaneer is a term usually applied to Caribbean pirates. It comes from the word *buccan*, which in the native Caribbean Arawak language means "a rack for drying meat." Originally, French sailors and hunters would occupy small islands and smoke the meat from feral pigs and cows that lived there, sometimes trading with ships. When the Spanish tried to drive the buccaneers from the islands, they joined forces with English and Dutch to retaliate, eventually becoming what we know today as pirates of the Caribbean.

The **corsair** was made famous by Lord Byron's poem about a handsome, brooding pirate. Corsairs were the pirates and privateers who operated primarily in North African and Mediterranean waters. They were also known as the Barbary pirates.

Long a staple of Hollywood, the **swashbuckler** got his name from *swash*, meaning to swagger (act or walk in an arrogant way), and from the *buckle*, a small shield popular at the time. The term is used for both pirates and swordsmen in general.

two

A Bloody Career Begins

Henry Morgan (sometimes known as Harry or Harri) was probably born in 1635 in Wales. He was from a moderately well-to-do family. His parents were likely farmers, but two of his uncles were prominent military men. One of them, Colonel Edward Morgan, served as lieutenant governor of Jamaica for a time. Members of his family fought on both sides of the English Civil War, some supporting the rebel Cromwell, others siding with the Royalists and the exiled King Charles II.

Morgan grew from a rural farmer's son to become one of the bloodiest pirates to sail the Caribbean.

Though raised in a farming family, Morgan had many relatives who were in the military, and who fought in the English Civil War.

A Self-taught Pirate

Morgan grew up in a military culture, and didn't have much use for school. Later in life he wrote of himself, "I left school too young to be a great proficient in that or other laws, and have been more used to the pike than the book." In the seventeenth century, a large portion of the population was illiterate. A young man of decent means might be expected to learn to read and write and do basic math, but not much more. When Morgan took to sea he probably learned the calculations necessary for ocean navigation, though he might have relied on a **pilot** specialist to travel. He was always more of a soldier than a sailor.

Morgan did have a sharp mind for strategy, however, no matter how limited his formal schooling might have been.

Pages from a Pirate's Life

Like many pirates, Morgan's childhood and early career are murky. His later life is fairly well documented, partly because of a biography about him that was written by Alexander Exquemelin, a barber-surgeon who actually served on Morgan's ship. Though Exquemelin provides valuable insight into Morgan's nature and his practices as a pirate, he had to rely on Morgan's word and his own limited research to uncover the events of Morgan's youth. Exquemelin also might have made his tales more dramatic, just to sell more books. One of his conjectures about the privateer's past provoked Morgan's extreme wrath, and also persisted through the centuries.

A 1655 entry in a log book listing servants sent to foreign plantations mentions one "Henry Morgan of Abergavenny, laborer, bound to Timothy Tounsend of Bristol, Cutler, for three years to serve in Barbados on the like conditions." Though there were many Welsh Morgans, and Henry was a very popular name, Exquemelin took this as proof that Morgan was sent to the Caribbean not as a free man but as an **indentured servant**.

Passage to the Caribbean

Many people, some who later found great success, first came to the Caribbean as indentured servants. Some were criminals who had a

Indentured servants sold themselves into virtual slavery for a fixed period of years. Though a biographer started a rumor that Morgan was once an indentured servant, he stoutly denied it.

prison (or even capital) sentence reduced in exchange for transportation. In the seventeenth century, a person could be executed for such relatively minor crimes as theft or counterfeiting. Other people sold themselves into servitude to pay off debts, or simply for passage to a new life in the New World. Some unfortunates were knocked unconscious at port towns such as Plymouth or Bristol, and woke up to find themselves prisoners on a ship sailing west, bound as servants for a fixed period. While indentured servants occupied a place in society above slaves, until they had worked off their debts they were still essentially owned by their masters. Most terms of indenture bound a person between three and seven years.

It is not likely that a young man of decent family, with relatives in high places in the military and government, would become an indentured servant. There is no known record of Morgan committing any criminal infraction at home that would have earned him such drastic punishment, and he probably could have immigrated to the Caribbean by his own means.

A Pirate, but a Gentleman, Too

Exquemelin's book, first published in Dutch, was later translated into Spanish and English. When Morgan read the English version, he was infuriated by the accusation that he'd ever been something as lowly as an indentured servant. He promptly sued the publishers of each edition for slander, and won an apology, revised editions, and £200 in damages from each publisher. The new version contained an introduction stating that Morgan was "a gentleman's son of good quality in the county of Monmouth, and never was a servant to anybody in his life, unless unto His Majesty."

Attacks on Caribbean Islands

However he got to the Caribbean, there is no confirmed official record of Morgan until 1655. Warlike from a young age, he joined a military force intent on capturing the island of Hispaniola when he was about twenty years old. Morgan had no experience as a sailor at that point. He was one of about seven thousand men who landed on the southern shore of the island and attacked the formidable Spanish defenses there. They were soundly defeated, not only by the Spanish, but also by bad leadership and devastating tropical diseases. (Morgan himself is said to have suffered from a recurrent tropical fever, possibly malaria, for most of his life.)

Later in 1655 that same army, humiliated and reduced in number, tried its skill against Jamaica. That island was much less fortified, and Morgan and the others overwhelmed the few Spanish soldiers there. Strategically located directly along two of the prime Caribbean trade routes, Jamaica became the center of England's hold on the region. Before long, the Jamaican town of Port Royal became a hub of trade—and piracy. Within a few years, Morgan had begun his bloody career as a privateer captain.

The islands of the Caribbean were the new center of colonial trade for England, Spain, and other European countries.

Alexander Exquemelin— Morgan's Surgeon Biographer

Alexander O. Exquemelin, probably a Frenchman who later settled in Holland, was hired by the French West India Company and sent to the Caribbean island of Tortuga. According to some other sources, he sold himself as an indentured servant to learn his trade. However he got to the Caribbean, Exquemelin trained under what was then known as a barber-surgeon. Like modern barbers, barber-surgeons could shave sailors but were also counted on to perform surgery, such as amputation. Without antibiotics or anesthesia, however, many patients died.

Exquemelin sailed with Morgan for several years, and was present at the attack of Panama. Despite the dismal survival rate for people undergoing surgery at this time, Morgan no doubt appreciated having a man with at least some medical training on his ship. Pirates and privateers were often injured during battle.

When Exquemelin returned to Europe, he promptly wrote about his experience with Morgan and his eyewitness accounts of other pirates. He first published it in Dutch as *De Americaensche Zee-Roovers*, but it was so popular that it was soon translated into German, Spanish, and French, and finally English as *The History*

Exquemelin paints a terrifying picture of the many tortures pirates used on their hapless victims.

of the Buccaneers of America. In it, he describes Morgan's acts of bravery, but he also spends a lot of time describing many barbaric acts. He tells of a pirate who ate the heart of one of his captives to intimidate the others into revealing their hidden treasure. Others, he said, would whip their victims, stretch them on a makeshift rack in the ship's rigging, or twist ropes around their head so tightly that their eyes popped out.

Exquemelin's book provides the best account of piracy we have today that was actually written at the time. His firsthand experience gave him a wealth of accurate knowledge, but he also made lots of mistakes with places and dates. It is also possible that, in order to ensure the success of his book, he made the deeds far more bloody than they really were. His main audience was Dutch and Spanish, and giving them further reason to hate the English privateer Morgan would spur them to buy the book.

three

The Terror of the Spanish Main

Morgan was the protégé of the leading pirate/privateer of the time, Edward Mansvelt, who was the chief of the buccaneers known as the Brethren of the Coast. For several years, Morgan took part in coastal raids on Spanish strongholds, learning his craft so well that he eventually captained his own ship. When Mansvelt was captured by the Spanish and executed in Havana, Cuba (though other sources say he simply died of a sudden illness), Morgan was his natural successor. He was elected Admiral of the Brethren of the Coast, the group of pirates and privateers in the Caribbean.

Morgan's first solo command was the attack on Puerto Principe.

What Did Morgan's Jolly Roger Look Like?

Jolly Roger is a term for the terrifying flags pirates flew. When a merchant ship saw that banner hoisted, they knew they were about to be attacked. One of the most famous pirate flags shows a white skull and crossed bones against a black background. Others featured crossed swords, skeletons, or devils. Some had a blood-red background. What did Morgan's pirate flag look like? This is a trick question!

Since Morgan operated more or less within British law with his letter of marque, Morgan's ships flew a variation of the British flag flown by the royal navy. Even though people of other nationalities, such as French or Dutch, sailed with Morgan, he wanted there to be no doubt that he was attacking the Spanish as an Englishman.

Pillaging Portobello

In 1668, Morgan set his sights on the treasure port of Portobello in Panama. Gold and jewels from South America were brought over land to this town, and ships would anchor in the large, sheltered harbor to load the booty bound for Spain. The three forts that guarded Portobello were designed to thwart attacks from the sea. Morgan thought that if he staged a surprise attack from the land, he could take the forts.

With rousing speeches and the promise of mountains of gold for his crew, Morgan led 500 men in canoes to a beach a few miles from the town. Under cloak of darkness, they crept in, and took the city almost without any resistance. They gathered the terrified townsfolk in one of the churches and began to attack the three forts.

The first fort surrendered, but the more heavily guarded Santiago Castle refused. That is, it refused until Morgan had the ruthless inspiration to use the civilians as human shields. He rounded up women, children, old men, friars, and even the mayor, and marched them in front of his attacking pirates. The fort fired a single round of chain shot, so-called because it fired two cannonballs linked by the length of a chain, which killed one pirate and wounded two friars. After realizing what they would have to do to their own families and religious leaders to protect the fort, the Spanish soldiers surrendered. That night, Exquemelin said, Morgan and the other pirates "began making merry, lording it with wine and women." By the next day, the third fort was taken, and Morgan set about getting all the gold he could from this adventure.

Tales of Torture

Morgan always said that he treated prisoners, particularly women, fairly and gently. However, survivors of his attacks tell a different story. When he thought that the locals might be withholding money

Pirates rarely buried their treasure—
or saved any money at all. Most engaged
in wild parties after a battle until their
money all ran out.

and gold, Morgan and his men began to systematically torture them until they revealed the location. One woman was supposedly roasted alive. Another, Doña Agustin de Rojas, was placed in a barrel of gunpowder. The pirates then waved lit fuses near her face and threatened to blow her up if she did not cooperate.

In addition to the treasure found in Portobello, the pirates also demanded ransom for their prisoners. When they'd gotten all the money they could, they abandoned the town and returned to Jamaica, where they drank and gambled until they were nearly broke. Since pirates rarely held onto the wealth they captured for long, stories about buried pirate treasure are largely false. Most spent their loot right away. Morgan managed to save more than many of his cohorts, retiring with enough money to buy a large amount of land in Jamaica.

Demise of the HMS *Oxford*

Before long, the pirates were penniless and looking for another fight in order to get more money. Morgan let all the pirates and captains know he was going to lead another raid, and called them all to meet at Isla Vaca off the coast of Hispaniola. Eight hundred men and ten ships agreed to raid another treasure port, Cartagena. After making this decision, they celebrated with an unruly dinner that included the usual pirate pastimes of drinking and celebratory gunfire. Unfortunately, a spark from the gunfire ignited the gunpowder stored on the huge warship HMS *Oxford*. The ship exploded, and two hundred men aboard were killed. Only ten men, including Morgan, survived.

The Maracaibo Bluff

The loss of their biggest ship and so many men, as well as other mishaps, doomed Morgan's planned attack on Cartagena to failure. Instead, Morgan led them to the poorly defended Maracaibo, a city located in northwestern Venezuela. During the attack, Morgan was almost trapped in the Maracaibo lagoon by three Spanish warships. Surrounded, they couldn't fight their way out, so Morgan came up with a plan to trick the Spanish. He fitted an old merchant ship with logs made to look like cannons, and straw dummies dressed as pirates. Then he loaded the ship with as much gunpowder as he could spare and sailed it directly at the Spanish blockade. The few men aboard threw grappling hooks onto the biggest Spanish ship, the *Magdalena*, lit the fuses, and escaped. The *Magdalena* quickly burned, and another Spanish ship ran aground on a sandbar in its haste to escape. Morgan captured the last ship. Once again, he and his men survived to return to Jamaica with their plunder.

Fire was one of every sailor's biggest fears. A stray spark set Morgan's flagship alight and caused an explosion that killed nearly all the crew.

During this period there was often a conflict between England's policy at home, and its practices in the Caribbean. Spain and England were officially at peace in Europe, but the governor of Jamaica was still authorizing attacks on Spanish ships and cities. It could take two months or more for a royal order or letter to cross the Atlantic, and it was easy for local officials to ignore their king's command and act in whatever way they thought was in England's, or their own, best interests. After the Maracaibo raid, Morgan was told to cease raiding Spanish towns. For a while he enjoyed his vacation, building his estate and spending time with his beloved wife, Mary Elizabeth Morgan.

Soon, though, the Spanish began attacking English ships, and violence on the high seas resumed.

Plundering Panama City

Morgan was confirmed as Admiral and commander in chief of all ships in the Port Royal, Jamaica, harbor. This allowed him to attack any Spanish ship and to steal or destroy anything that might be a threat to Jamaica. In 1671, he gathered the biggest pirate fleet the region had ever known, made up of 2,000 men and thirty-eight ships. He then made plans to attack the Spanish port of Panama City on the Pacific Ocean.

To get there, his men would have to cross the narrow Isthmus of Panama, land that connects North and South America and separates the Caribbean Sea from the Pacific Ocean. First, they attacked the castle of San Lorenzo, which guarded the mouth of the Chagres River on the Caribbean coast. It was a fierce battle, with the loss of many men on both sides, but finally Morgan's pirates held the castle. Now that the cannons were in the pirates' control, they could safely journey deeper into Panama. Morgan and his men sailed into the dense jungle, first on warships, then on canoes, and approached the young, inexperienced soldiers manning the Panama City garrison.

By the end of that battle, more than 500 Spanish lay dead, while only fifteen of Morgan's men had been killed. The city leaders had come up with what they thought was a perfect plan to repel the invaders. They had two herds of oxen ready to be stampeded through the attacking pirates.

The famous illustrator Howard Pyle was fascinated with pirates. Here, he depicts Morgan's men sacking Panama City.

However, the oxen proved docile, and the pirates just waved them away while Morgan continued his attack.

Though his pirates captured the city, it was not the financial success Morgan had hoped for. The Spanish had hastily loaded their treasure onto a ship at the first sign of attack and set fire to the city. Just as during the sack of Portobello, Morgan's pirates tortured civilians to discover hidden gold. They found some, but in the end, the booty amounted to no more than about £30,000, or about £15 per man. The men were angry and disappointed. Some even accused Morgan of keeping an unfair share for himself. The barber-surgeon Exquemelin was one of them, and this anger might have influenced him to paint a less-than-flattering portrait of Morgan.

The Pirate Code

Pirates are often portrayed as completely lawless ruffians. In fact, most of them followed a strict code, known as the articles of agreement, while on board their ships. This set of laws was laid out by the captain and agreed on by all of the crew. Pirate ships were largely democratic in a time where democracy was uncommon. The crew all got a vote in important matters, such as where to attack next. They were also entitled to vote for their own captain.

The articles varied from ship to ship, but in general they spelled out acceptable behavior among the pirates, the penalties for crimes, and the rewards after a successful plundering mission. For example, drinking on the ship was sometimes forbidden, or else restricted to certain hours. No man could smoke below deck or carry an uncovered lantern, which was a sensible precaution on a wooden ship filled with gunpowder. Some articles specified a bedtime, such as saying that lights had to be out by 8 p.m. To help prevent fights, gambling was also forbidden. If pirates did have a conflict, they couldn't draw their weapons against each other until they were on land. Penalties for violations might include flogging, marooning, which meant leaving them on land somewhere, or even execution.

four

Pirate in Retirement

The residents of Jamaica were thrilled with Morgan's successful attack on Panama City, but Spain was outraged. King Charles II in England was placed in a difficult position. In 1672, Morgan was politely arrested and sent to London. He claimed he had never received word of any peace treaty. All of England was sympathetic to their hero of the Caribbean, and Morgan was never imprisoned. Instead, he spent two years technically awaiting his fate, a time when he was actually being entertained by many of the most important aristocrats at court. He even gave the king advice about how to improve Jamaica's defenses.

King Charles II of England was secretly pleased with Morgan's exploits, but had to pretend to be upset to keep the Spanish happy.

In the end, instead of being punished, Morgan was given a knighthood. Now known as Sir Henry Morgan, he was sent back to Jamaica to be lieutenant governor, the island's second-in-command. Though he was shipwrecked on the return voyage, losing the new cannons that he'd brought for Port Royal's defense, he finally returned to Jamaica a rich and important man. He never sailed as a pirate again.

His Own Man

Morgan was a better buccaneer than bureaucrat. He did not like attending meetings with government officials, instead preferring to drink and gamble. Still, when a French fleet seemed poised to attack Jamaica, his old strategic expertise returned. He activated the militia, built two new forts, and even sent out ships and crew to drag up the sunken cannons from his shipwreck.

The Tide Turns

By 1687, though, Morgan was a wreck of his former self. Years of heavy drinking had taken their toll, as had recurrent bouts of tropical fever. He might have also contracted tuberculosis while in England. He suffered from what was then known as dropsy, a swelling of the legs or other body parts that can be caused by heart disease. A doctor described him as "lean, sallow-colored, his eyes a little yellowish and belly jutting out." In the end, "his belly swelled so as not to be contained in his coat."

Medicine was not very advanced in the seventeenth century. Bleeding and blistering a patient were common remedies. Illness was said to have

Bloodletting was a typical treatment for many ailments in the seventeenth century. It was largely ineffective and often dangerous.

caused an imbalance in the body's "humors," or different kinds of bodily fluids. A doctor treated Morgan's swelling by covering him in a plaster made of water and clay. Despite, or perhaps because of, these treatments, Morgan, at age 53, died on August 25, 1688.

Farewell at Sea

Morgan's body lay in state at the King's House (also known as Government House) in Port Royal as friends and admirers paid tribute to his life. He was then placed atop a gun carriage and drawn in a slow procession through town, coming to rest at St. Peter's Church. As he was lowered into the ground, all of the ships in the harbor fired their guns in salute.

Morgan had lived a relatively long life, unlike most of the pirates who would come after him. Many perished in battle. Those who survived combat usually met their end on the hangman's gibbet, executed for crimes such as robbery, murder, and treason. Many pirates died while aboard a ship and were buried at sea. They would be wrapped in linen, weighted down, and sunk overboard, if there was the opportunity. Many more might just have been tossed overboard. It seems a fitting end for a seaman, and as it turns out, Morgan's bones were not destined to rest on dry land. In 1692, a great earthquake struck Jamaica, destroying Port Royal, killing thousands, and washing the graveyard where Morgan was buried into the sea. The pirate found his final resting place with his brethren in Davy Jones's locker, the grave of those who die at sea.

Reenactors pay attention to the exact dress and manners of a seventeenth century pirate.

Resuscitating the Myth

Now, more than three hundred years later, Morgan remains well known. Popular culture has made him into the iconic Caribbean pirate. People today picture him as a confident, successful swashbuckler.

Morgan has also appeared in numerous movies, books, and comics. He is mentioned in the *Pirates of the Caribbean* movies, and in the spin-off children's books, *Legends of the Brethren Court*. One of the best-known pirate novels, *Captain Blood* by Rafael Sabatini, is based on Morgan's life. Ian Flemming's James Bond tale *Live and Let Die* features the discovery of Morgan's hidden treasure. Some groups and clubs engage in pirate reenactments for mock battles, and for parades. Many of their participants choose Morgan for their inspiration.

In the Footsteps of a Legend

Morgan was among the last of the Caribbean privateers. Most of the men who looted and plundered after him were true pirates, private captains who attacked any potential source of booty regardless of nationality. Among them were such notorious names as Blackbeard, Calico Jack, and Black Bart. They would make good use of the terror their predecessor Morgan inspired, following in his bloody footsteps with adventures even more gruesome.

The Golden Age of Piracy in the Caribbean would continue through about the 1730s. After that, most European nations strengthened their navies to combat the threat. There would still be pirates in later years. In fact, there are still pirates today. Morgan set the standard for them all.

The Search for Morgan's Ships

Morgan lost several ships on the treacherous reefs during his attack on Panama City. In 2010, a team from Texas State University uncovered cannons, chests, and a segment of a ship's wooden hull near the Lajas Reef off the Panamanian coast. All early indications showed that it was a seventeenth-century wreck, and the location suggested that it might be one of Morgan's ships lost in the attack. It could even be his flagship, the *Satisfaction*.

Before the Texas State team could prove their hypothesis, they ran out of money. Luckily an outside donor heard about their project and contributed money to help the team continue the investigation. A documentary about their project, *The Unsinkable Henry Morgan*, was filmed and debuted at the Sundance Film Festival in 2013. Yet as the investigation continued, it became clear that the ship wasn't one of Morgan's.

The ship was loaded with full chests. The pirates wouldn't have carried full chests to their raid. They'd leave their ship empty of all but their weapons and the most basic supplies so they could carry home more treasure. The cannons and the size didn't quite

Divers from the Texas State University research team search for a ship they hope belongs to Morgan.

match, either. However, the ship was definitely sailing the seas at the same time Morgan was.

The wreck might not be from Morgan's ship, but it is from Morgan's world. The artifacts uncovered, which offer a fascinating glimpse into seafaring life in the seventeenth century, are housed in the museum Patronato Panamá Viejo, located in Panama City.

Magnetic scans have revealed a number of other possible wrecks along that stretch of reef. Morgan's ships are still out there, waiting to be discovered.

Timeline

Circa 1635   Henry Morgan is born in Wales.

1649   King Charles I is beheaded; Oliver Cromwell named Lord Protector of the Commonwealth of England.

1654   Morgan takes part in the attempt to capture Hispaniola.

1655   Morgan participates in the capture of Jamaica.

1660   King Charles II is restored to the English throne.

1668   Morgan leads a lucrative raid on the treasure port of Portobello.

1669   Morgan is almost killed when his ship explodes before the attack on Cartagena.

1670   With increased threat of Spanish aggression, Morgan is named Admiral and commander in chief of all the ships in Port Royal harbor.

1670–1671	Morgan leads a huge fleet of buccaneers in an attack on Panama City.
1672	Morgan is arrested and sent to England to await charges of violating a peace treaty with Spain. He is never imprisoned and is acquitted of all charges.
1674	Morgan is knighted, becoming Sir Henry Morgan. He is also named lieutenant governor of Jamaica.
1688	Morgan dies of a combination of alcoholism, swelling, lingering tropical fever, and possibly tuberculosis.
1692	Morgan's corpse is swept out to sea in a massive earthquake.
2010	Researchers from Texas State University explore a shipwreck thought to belong to Sir Henry Morgan. massive earthquake.

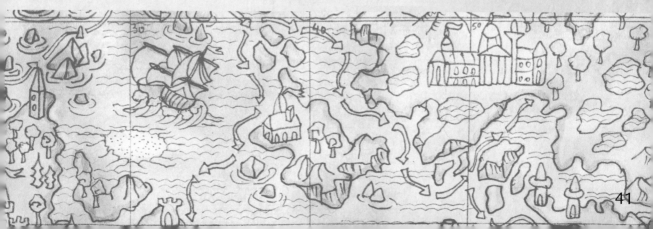

Glossary

able seaman In England's Royal Navy, a man who has at least two years of experience at sea. An able seaman could steer, sound for depth, and work aloft in the rigging.

articles of agreement Also known as the pirate code, this document set out the laws for behavior, discipline, pay, and compensation in case of injury.

booty Goods obtained by theft or violence; also known as loot or plunder.

buccaneer From the Arawak term *buccan*, which meant "a rack for drying meat," buccaneers began as hunters on Caribbean islands, and later became pirates.

colonial Relating to a land controlled by another country.

corsair Pirates and privateers who operated primarily in North African and Mediterranean waters; also known as the Barbary pirates.

flog To whip or beat as a punishment; a common method of discipline on a ship.

gallows A scaffold used during execution by hanging. It can also refer to any tree or other method of suspension used in a hanging.

Golden Age of Piracy The period from the 1650s to the 1730s when piracy flourished in the Caribbean, Atlantic Ocean, and elsewhere.

indentured servant A person who had sold themselves into debt bondage for a fixed term of years, agreeing to work in exchange for passage to another country. Some criminals were also held in indentured servitude.

letter of marque A license granted to a privateer authorizing them to attack enemy ships and share the profit with their government.

ordinary seaman In England's Royal Navy, a man who has between one and two years of experience at sea. Someone with less than one year of experience was called a landsman.

pilot An experienced ship handler who can guide ships through dangerous waterways.

pirate A person who, without authorization, attacks and plunders ships, or attacks the land from the sea.

privateer A person who, with such authorization as a letter of marque, attacks and plunders ships, or attacks the land from the sea.

Protestant Reformation The split in the Western European Christian community, in which some groups and nations left the Catholic Church and practiced Protestantism.

Spanish Main The coastal mainland of the parts of North, Central, and South America that were controlled by Spain.

swashbuckler A boasting violently active soldier, adventurer, or ruffian.

Find Out More

Books

Beahm, George. *Caribbean Pirates: A Treasure Chest of Fact, Fiction, and Folklore.* Charlottesville, VA: Hampton Roads Publishing, 2007.

Platt, Richard. *Pirate Diary: The Journal of Jake Carpenter.* Somerville, MA: Candlewick Press, 2005.

Steer, Dugald A., and Lubber, *Captain William.* Pirateology. Somerville, MA: Candlewick Press, 2006.

Websites

The Crimson Pirate

www.thecrimsonpirate.com/crimsonpirate.us

Explore the history of piracy dating back to more than 3,000 years. Learn about their lives at sea and on land, myths and punishments, view their photos, and read their individual biographies

Gentlemen of Fortune

www.gentlemenoffortune.com/index.htm

Reenact a pirate's life! Explore pirate ships, weapons, and even what they wore. Take a look at the ship's log for links to more pirate-related subjects.

Video

"The Unsinkable Henry Morgan"

www.youtube.com/watch?v=QZhfKpaCZWM

This Sundance Channel documentary explores the myths and legends surrounding Captain Henry Morgan's conquests in Panama.

Museums

The New England Pirate Museum

www.piratemuseum.com/pirate.html

Located in Salem, Massachusetts, this museum features a walking tour through the world of pirates, including recreations of a dockside village, ship, and a cave. Also on display are authentic pirate treasures.

The Pirates of Nassau

www.pirates-of-nassau.com/home.htm

Nassau was a pirate sanctuary for many years, welcoming Black Bart and many other noted pirates. This museum, located in the Bahamas, celebrates their exciting history.

The St. Augustine Pirate and Treasure Museum

www.thepiratemuseum.com

This interactive museum covers 300 years of pirate history, and boasts many artifacts including pirate loot, a real treasure chest, and one of only three surviving Jolly Roger flags.

Bibliography

Beahm, George. *Caribbean Pirates: A Treasure Chest of Fact, Fiction, and Folklore*. Charlottesville, VA: Hampton Roads Publishing, 2007.

Cordingly, David. *Under the Black Flag: The Romance and Reality of Life Among the Pirates*. New York, NY: Random House, 1995.

Exquemelin, Alexander. *History of the Buccaneers of America*. First edition published 1678. New York, NY: Digireads Publishing. Kindle edition.

Johnson, Captain Charles. *A General History of the Robberies and Murders of the Most Notorious Pyrates*. London, UK: Nathaniel Mist, 1724.

Konstam, Angus and Kean, Roger Michael. *Pirates: Predators of the Seas*. New York, NY: Skyhorse Publishing, 2007.

Pope, Dudley. *Harry Morgan's Way: The Biography of Sir Henry Morgan 1635–1684*. Cornwall, UK: House of Stratus, 2001.

Index

Page numbers in **boldface** are illustrations.

articles of agreement, 9, 31–32

Barbary pirates, **10**, 11
buccaneers, 5, 11, 21, 23

Caribbean, the, 6–7, 10–11, **13**, 15, 17–18, **19**, 20, 23, 28–29, 33, 36–37
Charles II, king of England, 5–6, 13, **33**
corsair, **10**, 11
Cromwell, Oliver, 9, 13

Exquemelin, Alexander, 15, 17, 20–21, 25, 30

Golden Age of Piracy, 7, 37

Hispaniola, 18, 27
HMS *Oxford*, 26–27

letters of marque, 9–10, 24

Mansvelt, Edward, 23
Morgan, Henry,
    and torture, 6–7, 21, 25–26, 30
    as a privateer, 9–10, 15, 18, **21**, 23, 37
    death, 5–6, 34–36
    early life, 13–25
    flags used by, 24
    in popular culture, 36–37
    knighthood, 5–6, 34
    retirement, 33–35

Port Royal, Jamaica, **8**, 18, 29, 34–36

St. Peter's Church, 6, 35
swashbucklers, 11, 36

Texas State University, 38–39

Unsinkable Henry Morgan, The, 38–39

About the Author

Laura L. Sullivan is a prolific author of books for children and young adults. Her novels include the fantasies *Under the Green Hill* and *Guardian of the Green Hill*, as well as the historical novels *Ladies in Waiting* and *Love by the Morning Star*. She is also the author of *Black Bart Roberts* and *Blackbeard* for Cavendish Square's True-Life Pirates series. She lives on the west coast of Florida, where she searches for buried treasure (even though she knows that pirates almost never buried their booty).